Girl Get A Grip: Business and Ministry Coaching Edition

# Girl Get A Grip

A Woman's Guide to

Moguling in Business

&

Thriving in Ministry

Volume 2

Francesca Stubbs

Francesca Stubbs

Girl Get A Grip: Life Coaching Edition

Copyright © 2017 Francesca Stubbs

ALL RIGHTS RESERVED.

This book is protected by the copyright laws of the United States of America This book may not be copied or reprinted for commercial profit or gain. The use of short quotations or occasional page copying for personal or group study is permitted and encouraged. Permission will be granted upon request. Unless otherwise noted, Scripture quotations are from the English Standard Version (ESV) of the Bible.

Published by SODAAN Publishing

A Subsidiary of
SODAAN Media & SODAAN Global, Int'l.
P.O. Box 229 Spring Lake, NC 28390

*"Publishing biblically sound, Apostolic and Prophetic resources for the Body of Christ."*

Copyright © 2017 Francesca Stubbs
All rights reserved.
ISBN13: 978-1976551772
ISBN-10-1976551773

Girl Get A Grip: Business and Ministry Coaching Edition

Girl Get A Grip: Business and Ministry Coaching Edition

# DEDICATION

This book is dedicated to the memories of two of the most important women in my life: My mother, Nicole Commodore and my grandmother, Frances Robinson. How I wish they both were alive today to see how their examples as strong women who handled their business no matter what obstacles they faced, paid off and caused me to become the woman that I am today. My resilient mentality and bulldog-work-ethic comes from both of you fabulous, tenacious women.

I love you both and miss you both beyond words. May my life leave a legacy that you both would've been proud of me for.

Also, to the memory of my precious older sister, Shawn, (Dinky) who lost her life to a violent act of domestic violence- this book is released on what would've been your 48$^{th}$ birthday. Even this book's cover is an homage to you- done in purple as an ode to you and others who have suffered any form of domestic abuse.

I celebrate your memory by sharing my gifts with other women hope of encouraging and spurring them on into their purpose, which will give them the confidence, courage and tools to live and succeed at birthing their dreams.
I love you and missed terribly.

Francesca Stubbs

Girl Get A Grip: Business and Ministry Coaching Edition

## CONTENTS

### Acknowledgments     I

### A Woman's Guide To Moguling in Business

| | | |
|---|---|---|
| 1 | Thrive | 14 |
| 2 | Dream It and Do It! | 20 |
| 3 | Beat Discouragement and Build | 26 |
| 4 | The Power of a Business-Minded Women | 32 |
| 5 | Business Mogul's Coaching Exercises | 38 |

### A Woman's Guide to Thriving in Ministry

| | | |
|---|---|---|
| 6 | Shattering Perspectives: The Woman Question | 46 |
| 7 | Virtue, Women and Reality TV | 54 |
| 8 | Keeping Your Heart Alive | 66 |
| 9 | Thriving Woman Coaching Exercises | 83 |
| | Bibliography | 87 |

Girl Get A Grip: Business and Ministry Coaching Edition

Girl Get A Grip: Business and Ministry Coaching Edition

## ACKNOWLEDGMENTS

This collection of work has special meaning all due to the love and support that I have received from my awesome family! To my husband, Javer, thank you for all of the encouraging words you have spoken to me during this process of birthing this book. I am forever grateful for how much you love me and have shown your support as I expand my boarders as an entrepreneur.

To my children, Jessica, Ijason, Javer Jr., and Francesca Darnelle, You are my biggest cheerleaders and a well of encouragement. Your words of love and support has propelled me forward and helped me to continue even when I thought I couldn't go any further. I love each one of you to the moon and back.

# Girl Get A Grip: Business and Ministry Coaching Edition

Francesca Stubbs

# A Woman's Guide

# To

# Moguling in Business

Girl Get A Grip: Life Coaching Edition

# 1
# THRIVE

*"The difference between successful people and others is how long they spend time feeling sorry for themselves."*
*Barbara Corcoran, Real Estate Magnate & Shark Tank Investor*

To thrive means to prosper and flourish, to burgeon, bloom, mushroom, to do well, advance, succeed, boom. These descriptions are great synonyms for the word drive notice in the subtitle of this book that this is a woman's guide to moguling in business and thriving in, ministry why do we need a guide for us to be able to thrive in business and ministry? First, you can be in business and in ministry and not be thriving. Many times, we are involved in different projects in life but that doesn't necessarily mean that we are thriving. I did business for several years and I did well I did okay. That does not mean that I was thriving. When I looked at this definition of thriving, I did some analyzing. Was I succeeding? Was I advancing in business? Not really. I had to learn different strategies and push myself to become better. The goal was to improve my business acumen and learn more about the areas of business that I was interested in.

I needed to be able to thrive- the same goes for ministry as well. I poured my heart out, gave my all. But I really wasn't thriving. that's a harsh reality to have the face-that you're doing something and not really thriving ...more like being in survival mode.

In order to thrive, you must first be able to determine what is your definition of thriving. Look at the definition given above. It means to succeed, to be prosperous, advance! What would advancement look like to you in your ministry or your business? Only you can answer these questions. Only you know how far you really want to go and how far you're willing to push yourself in order to achieve what thriving looks like for you.

Can you honestly say that you're happy with where you are now? Are you satisfied with your level of "success? "Or do you feel like there is more that you can achieve? More that you should become? More that you should be accomplishing? Then that means that you're not thriving! You must put your all behind this effort. It is will take everything that is in you to be able to thrive in your business.

No one else is going to do it for you. God is not coming down out of heaven to make you prosperous in what you are attempting to achieve. Nor is anyone going to do the hard work for you.

Are you honestly willing to put in the work necessary for you to be able to thrive in every area of your life? You must be honest with yourself. And since this is a coaching edition, part of my job as a coach is to be honest with you. You will never experience breakthrough. You will never experience success, or flourish if you do not put in the work. Settle it in your heart right now that everything that you aim to do to build your business, will be accomplished. Be determined that you will not just do it, but that you will thrive-that you will rock it out! That you will crush every goal that is before you. This must be your mentality! This is the only way you will be able to succeed.

### Dealing with obstructions

The only way that you're going to be able to thrive is for you to deal with your obstructions head-on. What are those things that are blocking you from being able to thrive? Is it that you don't really see yourself being successful at what it is that you're striving for? Are the rewards that have been spoken to you by friends, family members, or coworkers that seems to be stuck in the back of your mind and limiting your ability to move beyond what you have heard? can't move past it? Whatever it is that is blocking your view to success you need to remove it!

## Retraining Your Brain

Let's first start by retraining your thoughts about what it is that you think about yourself. You must understand that this is the most important thing. Not what other people think about you, but what you think about you. That matters. So, you must bring your thoughts into alignment with who you want to become. Previously we were talking about thriving now I want to talk to you about believing. Now we all believe something but what do you believe? Do you believe that you have the power to overcome every issue? Do you believe that you are powerful? Your faith in yourself and your abilities, is the key that unlocks your success and propel you forward.

Let's backtrack for a minute. I want to share a definition of what an obstruction is. Obstruction is a barrier, stumbling block, impediment, hindrance or snare. It could even be defined as a handicap or a restriction, it could be lawful or unlawful nevertheless it is still an obstruction. Looking at this definition, I'm led to ask what is it that is blocking you from thriving? You should be able to identify these pain points if you are going to become successful. As difficult as it may be, it must be done. Sometimes dealing with these "pain points" brings back the memories we must face, the issues we are struggling with, the people we've been rejected by, and most importantly the pain associated with each event. That is why it is called a "pain point". It is an entryway a source of what is hurting you and sometimes these obstructions though we may not realize it at first, but somewhere along the line, we have suffered a loss and/or injury. Financial loss is an injury to your personal economy. Sometimes, these kinds of losses cause of to be leery of taking risks. Doesn't it hurt for you not to be able to accomplish your goals? Isn't it painful when you look at where you are versus where you should be? Again, I say, you must deal with these obstructions. The best way to address them is head-on! That may mean having to go back to a previous employer or co-worker and ask someone to forgive you. You will also have to forgive them. It may also mean coming to terms with things that have happened in your past that were unsavoury, that you may have swept under the rug, and that you tried to just plain old forget about! Dealing with obstructions will make you face hard truths. It's not called "hard truth" for naught.

Let me encourage, you no matter how difficult it is to face and address your pain points, don't quit until they are obliterated. This may take you years or it could take you days. It all depends on how hard you're willing to work to get through these difficult places to thrive as you should. If you can get this right for yourself personally first, doing it for your business or your ministry or any other area of life is going to be a cakewalk. This is just the beginning. Now I want you to take a few minutes and jot down three of your most difficult pain points. List three things that are a constant obstruction to you and prevent you from thriving. Even if you think you may have more than three-however, I only want you to do the 1st three that come to your mind. List the ones that are the most difficult for you to deal with. If you deal with the most difficult problems first, I can assure you, swift breakthrough will follow in the areas that you need.

Now that you have dealt with your obstructions whether they were in your thoughts your emotions people past issues or whatever they may have been, you are ready to thrive in your life, business, and ministry!

Francesca Stubbs

## 2

## DREAM IT, DO IT!

*"Dear optimist, pessimist, and realist -- while you guys were busy arguing about the glass of wine, I drank it! Sincerely, the opportunist!"*
*Lori Greiner, Inventor, QVC host and Shark Tank Investor*

I want to take this moment to cause you to contemplate a few things. Ask yourself, am I where I want to be? Where did you say that you would be this year? Are you there? Have you done what you said you wanted to do? Why not? Where do you want to be six months from now? What do you want to be a year from now? Do you even know? In this chapter I want to address your dreams.

Are you spending a lot of time thinking about where you want to be and how you going to get there? That's dreaming. And there's nothing wrong with the dreaming, except if you don't do anything about what you're dreaming!

What does it mean to dream? To dream means to contemplate the possibility of doing something or becoming something. It is what you think about, it is what you consider and contemplate upon, it's a conception. It is a time of conceiving. That is what dreaming is.

What dreams will you have realized or manifested next year this time? How do you want your business to run? How much money would you like to make? Let me change or rephrase my question. How much money do you want to make? You must do more than just dream. You must do it! You must consciously think about your future. Never missing any opportunities. I want to take you through a few steps that are going to be helpful for you. It's something one of my mentors has help me with. This is a dream builder exercise. There are five steps to this exercise and I want you to follow them through let me coach you through manifesting your dreams. Dreaming and doing!

## Dream Building

**Step one:** take out a piece of paper and envelope. **Step two:** on the top of the piece of paper write "On (insert date exactly one year from today) I will... **Step three:** proceed to list out all the things you want to have an experience on that day. (EVERYTHING!)

Include the simple things like where you want to live and how you want to feel, then move on to what your day would look like, and how your business/career will be next, write those BIG, slightly scary but very THRILLING dreams you've never shared with anyone before. write as much or as little as you'd like. **Step four:** once you're done with your list, fold it up, put it in the envelope and seal it. **Step five:** on the outside of the envelope, write: "open on (insert date exactly one year from today") and put it somewhere safe. Then (guess what?) Open it on that day! There is so much power in you doing this and taking the time to speak to your future - speaking over your life- decreeing over yourself what you desire to become. It's setting up a time capsule that serves as notice to yourself that after you rock these plans and crush this goal that you can do anything! The only way that your dreams will ever become reality for you is, you must practice working on manifestation. If you do not all your dreams will continue to be just that, dreams! I am sure that you want to come out of dream mode and walk in Manifestation or else you would not be reading this book today. so, no matter where you are in your business today, or where you would like to be tomorrow, you have the ability to attain that goal. Your dream can be more than just a dream. You must dream it and you must do it! You can do it! You will do it!

## Dream Big!

Finally, as we are building our foundation on not just dreaming but doing, I want to emphasize to you how important it is for you to dream big. Dreaming big has everything to do with your ability and willingness to be a risk taker. Never underestimate the power of dreaming big. I'm a firm believer that if you can see it you can do it. So, what do you see? Are you ready to step out of your comfort zone and instead of dumbing down your dream are you ready to shoot for the stars? Why sit back and watch others as they accomplish their dreams and then think to yourself why couldn't I do that? You already know that you have the capacity to do great things. I will say that again. You already know that you have the capacity to do great things. Now repeat this phrase: "I already know that I have the capacity to do great things! This is why I must dream big. I am more than a dreamer, I am a doer!"

Don't think that you should have so much money or you must have the right people in your corner before you can really dream big. Mind you, we're talking about dreaming right? So before you see manifestation you dream. I want you to think about contemplate about meditate on what you desire to do and see yourself doing it on the largest scale possible. If you're thinking of starting your business and you want to be a coach see yourself coaching millionaires! See yourself being in demand! And when you begin to see yourself doing in a great way what it is that's in your heart that you desire, then you begin to act and think and walk out your dreams the way you have seen them. So essentially what I'm telling you is that your big dream becomes the archetype the blueprint for what it is that you become. So, if I'm dreaming big about starting my business, I am going to dream about where I want to be. Where do I want to live? How many people do I want on staff? All of that and more. If I'm going to see it, I first have to say it! If it's going to manifest, the vision has to first begin in my heart. My dream has to be, as we call it, in my mind's eye. Who is it that you want to be? What do you want to become? How great do you see yourself becoming? Dream big and do it big!

It doesn't matter what the highest level of your education is at this point in your life. You're not finished living! There's still more life for you to live, more for you to learn, and greater experiences to be had. one thing that will give you wings and help you to take flight is this: you are the only one that can prevent you from becoming great! No one else has the power to prevent you from dreaming big and becoming great! Remember that I asked the question, where do you want to be a year from now? Begin thinking of where you see yourself 10 years from now…20 years from now… Dream it! do it!

go after it! let nothing stand in your way, because dreams really do come true!

Girl Get A Grip: Business and Ministry Coaching Edition

Girl Get A Grip: Life Coaching Edition

# 3

# BEAT DISCOURAGEMENT. BUILD!

*"Don't be intimidated by what you don't know. That can be your greatest strength and ensure that you do things differently from everyone else."*
*Sara Blakely, Founder of Spanx*

There are times when the vision that we have in us and the manifestation we see before us just doesn't align. Once you set your heart to begin building your business, no matter what area of expertise it may be, there will be days that you feel as though nothing is working. Maybe at the onset, it's not too bad. Resistance is expected in the beginning so having to get over a few bumps when you first get going is not the problem. But what do you do when you have been toiling for months and it seems as though you are not making any headway? How do you handle the adversity of discouragement? Do you have a support system already in place? A mentor? Someone or a group that you can turn to that will help you regain perspective concerning your goals? These are all factors which must be considered as you engage in the process of setting up and building a successful business.

Discouragement defined in a nutshell is, [1]*a loss of confidence and enthusiasm, an attempt to prevent something by showing disapproval or creating difficulties; deterrent.* How many times have you felt deterred from your dream being fulfilled? How did you handle it? You will face difficulties daily as you are building but your determination to beat discouragement is what will make the difference between success and failure. Everyone will not believe in your dream. Stop expecting them to! It doesn't matter if those that are around you believe in what you are doing. You can't let their words get in your head! I know how important it is that your friends and family convey their faith in you and what you are doing, however, vision is for visionaries and everyone is NOT a visionary!

This is YOUR DREAM! Don't forget the zeal you had when you first started out. Go back and read the definition of discouragement again. I want you to be well versed on what it means and what it looks like, so that when you feel you have been hit by a ton of bricks and the wind is knocked out of you, the will to beat every deterrent and out-live every word of disapproval will be stirred in you to get up and keep building that business that you've always dreamed of.

## Planning Your Winning Strategy

Let's outline a strategy to win! If winning is indeed your goal, then you must always understand that NO ONE EVER WON BY ACCIDENT! Winning and those who win are intentional. They PLAY AND PLAN TO WIN! Now, that may not always be the physical outcome, however, intrinsic to every winner is the MENTALITY to keep going and WIN even though they have failings.

Thinking like a winner is the first step to beating discouragement. Yes, there will be times that you don't look like you are winning, but you don't have to stop there. The mindset to get up and keep building is a MUST if you are going to accomplish your goals, and build a successfully lucrative business. I want to share a list of things you can do as part of your strategy to beat discouragement.

- **Make Perspective Your Priority**. What and how you are thinking is key to your success. How do you see your situation? Try to focus more on your possibilities and the favorable options that present themselves and not the barriers and obstructions that you have encountered.
- **Change Your Vocabulary**: What are you saying to yourself? Self-talk is a very important issue when it comes to achieving your goals and beating discouragement. It is one thing for an individual to speak negatively to you, it is an altogether different situation, a death-blow if you are

speaking negativity to yourself, your dreams and endeavors.
- **Be Tenacious**: How well do you know that field you are embarking upon? Set your mind to be tough and develop a Pit-bull mentality as it pertains to your business goals. Be unwilling to give in no matter how many difficulties you may face. Doors may close-but rest assured, many other will swing wide open!
- **Do The Hustle**: This means you have to push your brand, product, business like there's no tomorrow. You are the celebrity of your brand, therefore, you need to be prepared to hustle baby! If you're going to be successful, you can't be afraid to get out there and do your thing. It may be hard in the beginning but the end result and reward of success will all be worth it when you're on your way to the bank!
- **Discipline Yourself**: Stay focused and don't allow yourself to lose sight of what your main objective is. The daily "hustle" can be taxing at times and the temptations to go off on tangents and start a new venture before you complete the one you are currently building is a true reality. In the grand scheme of things, it is very important that as a business owner and visionary, that you keep your emotions under control and stick with the plan no matter what. Plan times for development as a business owner and entrepreneur. Make sure you have an accountability partner, business-mentor, or coach that can keep you honest about where you are and what is going with you at any given time. This will prove to be invaluable as you progress in you endeavors and ensure that you remain on-task, goal-focused and result-driven for your business.

## Step Up

Now that you understand discouragement and have a strategy to keep you on target, let's focus on a vital key to winning as a business owner and being a successful mogul in the era in which we live and the field you are working in. Step-up and come to the table! This is one the vital keys to you obtaining successful results. Learn to be ready at any given time to step-up and take your seat at the table you've been called to; even if you don't feel prepared! Don't allow the lack of mastery in an area prevent you from letting the world know that you are present and ready to go for it. You can always get the tools you need once you get your foot in the right door, meet the right people, or get the adequate capital you need to build your business. However, opportune times can be fickle and unseasonal, therefore, always be ready to state your claim for the prize of success. It doesn't matter if you have to conjure up a last minute elevator-pitch. Always be prepared because great things can come your way even on days that you are the least prepared. You have to be ready and willing to jump at a moment's notice, to take risks, speak up, and talk up your business like it's the best thing since sliced bread! Be courageous. Be ready and use everything in your arsenal to push your dreams forward. Doing so and remaining consistent, you will triumph and flourish and YOU WILL beat discouragement!

Girl Get A Grip: Business and Ministry Coaching Edition

Girl Get A Grip: Life Coaching Edition

# 4

# THE POWER OF A BUSINESS-MINDED WOMAN

*"Define success on your own terms, achieve it by your own rules, and build a life you're proud to live." -- Anne Sweeney, Walt Disney*

I want to begin this chapter by placing a heavy emphasis on the power of a business-minded woman. Being a business owner for any individual male or female is difficult, however, I believe that a woman brings something very unique to the table. Along with her femininity, there is a strength that she brings to any corporation. Whether she is the CEO or if she's the administrative assistant.

While many are walking the beat, trying to find a job in the conventional sense, strong women are starting their own businesses daily. This is an awesome time in which we live that women can begin their own businesses with the gifts and talents that they possess. The possibilities are endless.

Never before have we seen such a resurgence of new businesses and industries being created with many of them being spearheaded by women.

"[2]A recent SBA office of advocacy report on women's business ownership described women entrepreneurs as an "economic powerhouse" the report, based on the most recent data from the US Census Bureau offers some impressive data: women own 9.9 million businesses in the US; women employ more than 8 million workers; women provide more than $264 billion in wages and salaries to employees; and women owned businesses contribute $1.4 trillion in sales to our national economy"

The statistics above reiterate how powerful a business-minded woman really is. Let's just look at what exactly women bring to the workplace looking at the statistics from the article above shows us that women business owners are making major contributions to society today. Women are strong, tenacious, and also very witty and intelligent. With access to mentoring programs, education and internships, the possibilities are endless for women in business. There is no such thing as a glass ceiling anymore! It has already been shattered. The only thing left for us to do as women is to get out and do what is in our heart to do which is start businesses. Women are taking advantage of educational and professional opportunities, forging forward into entrepreneurial waters likes sharks after prey, and they are winning at it!

## The Power of Support

This is of utmost importance. Every woman should receive the support that is needed in order for them to embark upon their new careers. Long gone are the days of just selling cookies and having bake sales! These powerhouse women are opening restaurants and bakeries, starting Fortune 500 companies, sitting at the desk as CEO and CFO's and heading multimillion dollar organizations. What type of support do you think these gifted business women need? These powerhouses need to be able to connect with other role models who like them, are women in business. They need to be able to have mentors who are in their fields of expertise who will train them and help them along their journey as they are climbing the corporate ladder. For those of us who are building businesses, having mentors who are successful entrepreneurs assists new business owners avoid pitfalls that are common to fledgling entrepreneurs. There are many discouragements that a company starting a new business venture may encounter. However, the advantages of connecting with women who are tenacious and strong-minded will assist in the building of the same virtues in those that are being mentored.

## Tough It Out

It is very important that you set your heart and your mind to tough it out. There will be days that you may run out of capital, and out of ideas. But you must never run out of resilience! You must always continue to press forward for the success of your business.

One of the areas that is very important for women in business to stake their claim on is raising up other business women. As mentioned before, mentoring is a very big component for success. Just as you as a business woman needs to have a mentor, you also should be speaking into the lives of other business women who are coming up behind you.

In church we call them spiritual mothers. These are women who take the time to nurture, encourage, correct, train and instruct other younger women that are coming up behind them. In like manner, we need the same tool of training in the business community. Having a business mentor or a business-mentoring-matriarch makes all the difference in your success as a business woman. Think of all of your skills all and talents that you have, as well as all of the gifts you possess that you bring to the table.

Whether it is starting a daycare center, school, computer software company, a radio broadcasting company or whatever it is that is in your heart to do, you bring your unique flavor to the world when you open up your business. There will be people who are waiting for you. There are lives that you're going to touch and impact, all because you bring your unique flavor into the boardroom.

It may take some time to build your business to the pinnacle of your dreams; but while you are building, use every tool you have acquired and work every skillset that you possess-all while standing in your power as a business-minded woman.

Girl Get A Grip: Life Coaching Edition

Francesca Stubbs

## Business Mogul's Coaching Journal

*"I just love bossy women. I could be around them all day. To me, bossy is not a pejorative term at all. It means somebody's passionate and engaged and ambitious and doesn't mind leading." -- Amy Poehler, actress*

Girl Get A Grip: Life Coaching Edition

# 5
# BUSINESS MOGUL COACHING EXERCISES

## Chapter 1
## Thrive

**Write a brief, detailed description of what thriving in business looks like to you?**

_____
_____
_____
_____
_____

**Can you say that you are happy with where you are professionally today? Explain.**

_____
_____
_____
_____
_____

**List three of your most difficult "Pain Points"**

_____
_____
_____

**List 3 obstructions that hinder you from thriving and how you plan to overcome them.**

_____
_____

## Chapter 2 Dream It! Do It!

What do you dream of doing? Have you begun manifesting this dream? If not, how will you manifest this dream?

What is the biggest/scariest dream you've had? What are you doing about it?

## Chapter 3
## Beat Discouragement: Build!

In what ways has discouragement presented itself as you are building your business? Share at least 2 examples.

How will you apply the strategies shared in this chapter to beat discouragement when it comes?

_____
_____
_____
_____
_____

Have you ever been called "to the table" and faced discouragement? Did it prevent you from jumping into an opportunity? Explain.

_____
_____
_____
_____
_____

## Chapter 4
### The Power of a Business-Minded Woman

What is your personal definition of a powerful woman? What does she look like to you?

_____
_____
_____
_____
_____

Do you have a business mentor or a Business-Mentoring-Matriarch?" If so, describe her impact in your life. If not, share what area you feel a mentor would be most helpful.

In your opinion, what is your "unique flavor" that you bring "to the table" in business? List at least 5 things.

List the tools that you are using/will use to secure a successful business future.

Francesca Stubbs

# Girl Get A Grip: Business and Ministry Coaching Edition

Francesca Stubbs

## Girl Get A Grip

## A Woman's Guide

## to

## Thriving in Ministry

# 6
# SHATTERING PERCEPTIONS: THE WOMAN QUESTION

'Like fish, we "swim" in a sea of images, and these images help shape our perceptions of the world and of ourselves.' (Berger, 2008)

We will begin this subject by first looking into the Scripture.

John chapter 8:3 says, "the scribes and the Pharisees brought a woman who had been caught in adultery," Isn't it funny they bring the woman who was caught in adultery, but where was the man? " and placing her in the midst they said to him, teacher this woman has been caught in the act of adultery. Now in the law of Moses commanded us to stone such women. so what do you say? This they said to test him that they may have some charge to bring against him. Jesus bent down and wrote with his finger on the ground. And as they as they continued to ask him, he stood up and said to him to them, let him who is without sin among you be the first to throw a stone at her. And once more he bent down and wrote on the ground. But when they heard it, they went away one by one, beginning with the older ones and Jesus was left alone with the woman standing before him. Jesus stood up and said to her, woman where are they? Has no one condemned you? She said no one, Lord. And Jesus said, neither do I condemn you; go, and from now on sin no more."

Look at what Jesus was doing in vss. 3-11. You have to understand that not only was Jesus forgiving stand for God to forgive sin that is not a big deal because that is his nature to forgive. God is a forgiving God, but what Jesus was doing? He was shattering perceptions about women. He was shattering the mindsets of what the people thought about women in that day.

It is ironic how this all unfolds. With all the that's going on in the church-world these days- such as women becoming Bishops and Apostles, (myself included.) The whole woman question coming up again, doesn't surprise me. I had just finish teaching (I was teaching two classes), and we had just finished our second week, In our second week of classes, we discussed the subject of women in authority, apostolic women and women in ministry. I was also teaching about the issues that surround the woman question. I was in disbelief when I was approached about this again. My thought was, "are you kidding me? Are we back at this again?"

I'm fully aware that this issue has been going on in the church for centuries. My dilemma began when I listened to a very prominent minister who was born again and trained for ministry by a female pastor, stand and denounce women in ministry! It's unbelievable! How could you possibly denounce women being pastors and leaders when you were born again in a church lead by a woman? It makes no sense to me! However, this leader was allowed to make this claim and no one call him on the carpet about his erroneous doctrine. My question to that particular minister who now decries women in ministry would be, was your salvation experience real? What about all the things that you were taught in that ministry growing up? Can you believe those things? How did you once believe something and now that you have a major platform, you denounce your former belief to the detriment of those women who are now following your ministry?

He is clearly contradicting himself without really realizing what he is doing. Every one of us needs to learn the art of becoming theologians because we are studying the scripture that is our responsibility- that we might be able to give an answer to every man for the faith that lies in us.

Now, let's get back to my first point. Jesus is shattering perceptions. Notice what it says in the 31st verse of this chapter: "if you do what I say, if you follow my words, then you are my disciples." Then he said, "if you abide in me and if you abide in my word, you are truly my disciples; and you will know the truth and the truth will make you free." That means that these believers thought they knew the truth, but what they. believed was not truth at all! Jesus said, they would know the truth, when you know what the truth is, it is going to make you free! Jesus had to shatter the perception that women were unclean, evil, and inferior. Clearly, that is what they believed, but is could not be further from the truth!

Jesus was shattering this perception! Now the fact that he was even speaking to this woman is a major event. And we are also aware of the fact that the woman didn't commit adultery by herself ...where was this man she had been with? We all understand that the man who participated in the sin with the woman mentioned in the verses that we read should have been present to face his accusers and receive judgment as well. This fact made room for Jesus to deal with the perceptions of the culture. These men thought that women were evil and unclean or else they wouldn't have been prepared to deal with her in such an unjust manner.

This was the pervasive thought pattern that permeated throughout the culture. You cannot receive an accurate understanding of the Scriptures by doing a surface study of the verses we've read. You must include in your study, the historicity of the Scriptures when you read in the Bible. We must note the context of the text in question. A good rule of thumb to remember is text out of context no text at all. The next item to consider is the pretext. These must all be taken into account when seeking understanding of Scripture. The fact that many draw conclusions without following the steps above, is the reason we find so many erroneous doctrines that have been adopted by the church. When you go to Bible College, you have to study Manners and Customs. If you've never studied Manners and Customs of the Bible, please take a minute and go to the library and get the book. Look it up online. You can get a copy of Manners and Customs of the Bible from any bookstore and be able to decipher the traditions.

This brings me to another point. Jesus was shattering traditions and beliefs that taught that the woman was responsible for many of the wicked things that were taking place. When I hear people talking and they go back to the book of Genesis and they say. "the Bible says that Eve sinned first." My response is, the curse didn't come just because she sinned. The curse was pronounced because both Adam and Eve sinned. God's creation sinned and because of that, they both suffered the consequences. If the woman was not responsible for anything, and her position inconsequential, there would have been no reason for God to make her suffer judgment of the curse along with Adam. It's a simple deduction! You don't have to be a scholar to come to the conclusion that only responsible parties are held accountable for their actions. If Eve's (the woman's) position is so much lessor in value, power, position and authority, why wasn't she absolved of her wrong-doing and only Adam held accountable for transgression of God's commandment? That's a good question, isn't it? It's because they both (Adam and Eve) were given dominion and ruled equally in the Garden of Eden and therefore, they were jointly and individually guilty of transgressing -which meant they both were to be punished EQUALLY!

If what I have stated above is not the case, and if woman is indeed inferior to man, then she should not be held accountable for the choice she made, nor should she have faced being cursed. The truth is that God was showing that even in His pronouncing judgment on them both, that women were equal in substance, equal in authority and value.

Let's look at this in the book of Matthew. You need to read this for yourself. Before we look at the verses, please understand, Jesus lived in a "man's world." This was what is called a Patriarchal Society. This means that men were in authority over women in every aspect of life and function. Not only so, but women were thought of as property and didn't have the same rights, privileges and authority as men. Women who lived during the period of time when Scripture was written, in fact, had no voice. However, as you read the Gospels, you will see that woven throughout the Scripture, Jesus gave women a voice; even though it was not an acceptable practice.

To add a quick sidebar note, I want to bring into the picture Feminism and what it really is and where it originated. The best thing to do is to begin with a dictionary and to define what Feminism is. So let's start there. [3]*Feminism-the advocacy of women's rights on the basis of the equality of the sexes.* The reason we need to unearth this terminology is due to the fact that many Believers are under the assumption that

Feminism and the Feminist movement originates from some demonically inspired individual. In fact, the Women's Suffrage Movement was spearheaded by Believing women who stood against the injustices that were committed against them, solely because of their gender. Prophetically, we are still here and this issue, though not as harsh as it once was, still needs addressing so we turn to the Scripture so that we can learn from Jesus as he elevates women and shatters the prevailing perceptions of that era by speaking to them, giving them commands, forgiving their sins, allowing them to be His followers and defending them even when they have been caught in sin by the very men that sought to keep them subservient.

It is of utmost importance, as I have already stated, that we understand the historicity, pretext, context, and post-text of the Scripture so that we are able to read and understand accurately what is being stated, to whom it is stated and how it should be interpreted. The Bible instructs us to *"Study to show thyself approved unto God, a workman that needeth not to be ashamed, rightly dividing the word of truth.: (2 Tim 2:15, KJV)* Now that we have dealt with that, we can finally go to Matthew as planned.

> Look at Matthew 9:20-22; *"And behold, a woman who had suffered discharged of blood for twelve years came up behind Him and touched the fringe of His garment, for she said to herself, "If I only touch His garment, I will be made well." Jesus turned, and seeing her He said, "Take heart, daughter, your faith has made you well." And instantly, the woman was made well."*

What was Jesus doing here in the verses we just read? First of all, this woman, who was already deemed unclean according to the Law, risked her very life-crawling through the thronging crowd to touch Jesus for her healing. Not only was she already ceremonially unclean, she contaminated every person in the crowd she pushed against in her pursuit of healing! If they had known that this unclean vessel was in their midst, purposely defiling others just to get to Jesus, they would have most certainly had her stoned! Now, seeing this through the eyes of a Hebrew people, who knew the Law and some in the crowd who no doubt knew the medical history of this woman, Jesus proceeds to 1. Speak to her, and 2. heal her instead of rebuking her and having her immediately brought to judgment for stoning!

Now, back to the question at hand, what was Jesus doing? The obvious answer is that He was healing the woman with the issue of blood. More importantly, if we look deeper into the facts that have been previously shared before we read this text, we will see the real motive and power behind the gesture toward this woman. For those reading this who are nor well-versed with the Law of Moses, this woman was considered "unclean", (Leviticus 15:19); So again, what was Jesus doing when He healed this woman? He was removing the perception that women were unclean! When Jesus forgave the woman caught in adultery, He was making a statement and delivering her from the cultural perception that women were evil! (John 8:1-11). Jesus deliberately did these miracles in public to heal the societal perceptions that prevailed during that time and to show them openly that He was a champion for women; that the new way He was introducing, though new to them, showed the love, compassion and care God has for women and that femininity was to be celebrated, not bashed and shunned.

The importance of this is far beyond one culture. Our perceptions, even today, must be adjusted due to the fact that what we perceive dictates how or if we are able to receive. So, if women are to be treated as second class citizens, how then can she carry the Gospel and bring glory to God? How then can she start a business and even dream of being slightly successful when she is already frowned upon at the threshold of the door of opportunity? It is impossible! Therefore, it is of utmost urgency that we navigate through the Scripture with proper perspective and look deeper than our commentaries to see the heart of our Lord and interpret His actions in such a way that we are able to see the great revelation that is hidden behind His every action as He lifted, praised, encouraged and released the woman from the bondages of faulty perceptions of the men in the society in which she lived.

It is noteworthy to add that there is a direct correlation between the perceptions of women and how society receives from them, and even the result of how females will view themselves as women. It is impossible to separate the ideologies of a culture from the behavior and perceptions that are born as a result of them. Culture has the power to influence every facet of our lives; thoughts, behaviors, dress codes and it even determines what we deem as acceptable and normal as a people. Hence, the message and ministry of Jesus, as a counter-cultural hammer, swinging in polar-opposite of the socially acceptable norms; freeing women from the bondage of the pasts short-sighted and prejudicial chains.

If we are to properly raise sons as well as daughters with a healthy understanding and appreciation of women and womanhood, we must first pull down the strongholds that yet prevail; not only in archaic societies, or third-world countries who seem behind the times, but also, right here in the United States of America- in the year 2017! There is still a struggle and overarching thought that has intermingled with modern culture and beliefs today. These beliefs state that women are in some way inferior or unequal to men and that this one gender of humanity is the purveyor of many of the woes of our society.

We see it in television programs every day. Women are portrayed as witches-even to our children (Disney's Cruella D'Ville); or they are the quintessential housewife who looks perfect on the outside, yet she is a wonton seductress who seeks sexual gratification outside her marriage covenant, (ABC's Desparate Housewives).

Our responsibility as Believers is to search the Word of God for the Truth and to share it with others that they may walk in liberty, continuing the ministry that Jesus began. As we faithfully do our part and teach others, we too, will shatter the perceptions in our society by answering the woman question.

# 7
# VIRTUE, WOMEN, AND REALITY T.V.

I would like to spend begin this chapter being very direct because there seems to be a dilemma in the church today. We have lost the desire to be virtuous women in exchange for a Hollywood persona. The world is not the only one driven by high-fashion and commercials that tell us we need to buy everything we see, because "we need it." The church, namely, women in the church have been seduced and overtaken by commercialism and blatant sexual prowess.

Let's begin by reading the following verses:

Proverbs 31:10-31 (KJV)
*Who can find a virtuous woman? for her price is far above rubies. The heart of her husband doth safely trust in her, so that he shall have no need of spoil. She will do him good and not evil all the days of her life. She seeketh wool, and flax, and worketh willingly with her hands. She is like the merchants' ships; she bringeth her food from afar. She riseth also while it is yet night, and giveth meat to her household, and a portion to her maidens. She considereth a field, and buyeth it: with the fruit of her hands she planteth a vineyard. She girdeth her loins with strength, and strengtheneth her arms. She perceiveth that her merchandise is good: her candle goeth not out by night. She layeth her hands to the spindle, and her hands hold the distaff. She stretcheth out her hand to the poor; yea, she reacheth forth her hands to the needy. She is not afraid of the snow for her household: for all her household are clothed with scarlet. She maketh herself coverings of tapestry; her clothing is silk and purple. Her husband is known in the gates, when he sitteth among the elders of the land. She maketh fine linen, and selleth it; and delivereth girdles unto the merchant. Strength and honour are her clothing; and she shall rejoice in time to come. She openeth praised.Give her of the fruit of her hands; and let her own works her mouth with wisdom; and in her tongue is the law of kindness.*

*She looketh well to the ways of her household, and eateth not the bread of idleness. Her children arise up, and call her blessed; her husband also, and he praiseth her. Many daughters have done virtuously, but thou excellest them all. Favour is deceitful, and beauty is vain: but a woman that feareth the Lord, she shall be praise her in the gates.*

## Faulty Reality

We have pews full of women, but we can't say that they all are virtuous. Unfortunately, we have a problem with watching too much reality television. Reality television really isn't our reality; it's someone else's reality. Here it is, Solomon is being spoken to by his mother, Bathsheba. She is telling him what to look out for because she knew the type of woman she once was. She remembered all too well what happened as result of her bathing on top of her house in the morning when everybody was at home. She understood what she needed to tell her children. Isn't it true that we know how to tell our sons and daughters what to look for in a companion?

When we look in our churches, we are finding out that the women in the church are acting like the Real Housewives of Atlanta. We have a problem in that this is what the world is putting out there, and we don't have sense enough not to repeat it. If Solomon is being asked who can find a virtuous woman, this means that virtuous women are not found as often as we need to find them. We are preoccupied with other things. It is unfortunate that some of us will go to church and shout and dance after we just left the club or jumped out of someone else's bed. We will come to church after we just finished hugging up or smooching with someone we had no business hugging up or smooching with. We do all of that and then want to come to church and call ourselves virtuous. Not so.

First of all, she says to him that "her price is far above rubies." You can't even put a price on a real virtuous woman. Her value exceeds that which you can pay for. When you find a real good woman, you can't buy her. It doesn't matter how many cars you have or how much money you have. It doesn't matter if you try to take her to dinner or take her to some fancy hotel because you want to try to get your groove on or whatever - none of that is going to allow her to lose her virtue. Now I know you know what I'm talking about. If you don't, just pray for me. Verse eleven says that *"The heart of her husband doth safely trust in her, so that he shall have no need of spoil."* Our husbands should know that they can trust in us. If you are married, Jesus is your husband, and He should be able to trust you. This means that you should not be laying down with anyone that you are not married to. It means that you are going to be saved when you come to church and saved when you walk out the door. When I leave the house, my husband isn't worried about where I'm going. He's not having to ring my phone and ask me where I am and who I'm with. He doesn't have a fear of me smooching up with somebody else. He knows what he's got. Our husbands should know what they have. Those of you who aren't married need to know that God knows what He's got in you. You should be able to carry yourself as a godly woman.

## Wanton Women

Let's talk about a few things concerning godly women. We have to learn how to cover some things up. Even concerning the mothers, we don't know if they are mothers or what they are because of how they are dressed. We come to church and the mothers of the church are trying to pick up the young men in the church. We've got cougars in the church, and that makes no sense! We can't trust our young men in the church because Mother So & So is trying to pick them up. Mother is wearing her skirts as short as she can wear them and her chest is hanging out. That's not right! You should be able to be trusted. Can anyone trust you? Can we trust you to be a mother? It's the truth anyhow. I've seen it. It's enough to make you sick. This is still the gospel anyway. Even if people don't want it to be preached. It's the truth anyhow. God said that His house shall be called the house of prayer, but we have made it a den of thieves (Matthew 21:23). Some people aren't stealing money but they are stealing the hearts and the souls of men.

Verse twelve says that *"She will do him good and not evil all the days of her life."* Though my husband gets on my nerves, I'm not going do him any evil. I'm not going to engage in wickedness to get back at him. I might think about it but I'm going to rebuke it. Don't act like you're so sanctified that you don't think about getting back at folks. You know that's the truth! Verse thirteen says that "*She seeketh wool, and flax, and worketh willingly with her hands.*" She's not a lazy woman. There's nothing worse than being lazy. Nobody can rely on you because you're lazy. We call your house at 1:00 in the afternoon and you're still in the bed? You're lazy. We have to learn how to get up out of the bed and be about our Father's business. This is talking about a woman who finds a way to do what she needs to do and as a result, her husband will be praised. It's hard for some of us to do something for someone else to get the glory for all of our hard work. How do you feel when you do something and someone else gets the credit? We feel slighted. We like to receive our little applause.

## An Industrious Woman

The Bible says in the fourteenth and fifteenth verses that "She is like the merchants' ships; she bringeth her food from afar. She riseth also while it is yet night, and giveth meat to her household, and a portion to her maidens." I told you that she's not in the bed at 1:00pm. We have to be industrious. It is the will of God that we as women learn how to make good use of our time. Instead of us being on the phone and Facebooking all day long, we need to be using our time to do the will of God. I'm sure that God deals with all of us about making sure that we have time in prayer, time in the word, time to take care of what needs to be taken care of at home, and time for ministry. You have to have time for these things, and you can't do that if you're in the bed all day. Now don't get me wrong: I have days in which I sleep in. I'm not saying that you can't have a day to sleep in. I'm not saying that you can't have a chill day. But every day can't be your chill day. You can't have so many chill days that you don't even know what day it is.

Verses sixteen and seventeen tell us that *"She considereth a field, and buyeth it: with the fruit of her hands she planteth a vineyard. She girdeth her loins with strength, and strengtheneth her arms."* I need to tell you that there's not always going to be someone to come along and speak strength to you. You're going to have to learn how to speak strength to yourself. You're going to have to learn to strengthen your own arm. You will have to learn how to speak life to yourself when you feel like you're dying or already dead. Strength is her girdle. It's what holds her together. When she feels like falling apart when life is getting on her nerves, and when it seems like all hell is breaking loose, she has something on the inside of her that's helping her to stay and stand. It used to be that praying women had some stamina about themselves. You wouldn't see strong women of God backsliding every five minutes. I know we go through and I know we have circumstances that come against us. I know that there are things we must experience, but can you stay saved for forty-eight hours? Can you hold on to Jesus for more than an hour of service so that when you leave we don't have to have prayer with you again?

Verse eighteen says, "*She perceiveth that her merchandise is good: her candle goeth not out by night.*" I don't need you to come and tell me that what I made is good. You don't need your neighbor to come and tell you that what you made is good. You should already know it's good, and you should be industrious and go make money from it. It used to be that women would do whatever they had to do so that their families would be able to make it. Where are those women today? They wouldn't let the sun go down before they handled their business. While everybody else is in the bed and going to sleep, the virtuous woman is seeking the Lord. She's trying to find out what God wants her to do. She's asking God for instruction and direction. Where are the women who are intercessors that will get on their faces before the Lord? Where are the women who will burn the midnight oil? It's alright for us to come to church and look cute. I like my makeup, my high heels and all of that, but there has to be more to us than that. I believe that this life we are living is going to require that we have more than a cute face and a pair of pumps. You'd better have something in your inner man. You'd better have some strength in your girdle. You'd better be able to take something. You have to know how to go through and endure. You have to be able to pray through. Even if you feel like giving up, you'd better not give up.

We learn in verses nineteen and twenty that "*She layeth her hands to the spindle, and her hands hold the distaff. She stretcheth out her hand to the poor; yea, she reacheth forth her hands to the needy.*" In other words, she's not just concerned about "me, my, and mine". Her heart is on those who are in need. She's not selfish. She's not just concerned about making herself and her family only. She's a good neighbor. Once upon a time we had some godly women who were good neighbors. I should be concerned about my sister who's sitting next to me. She shouldn't even have to tell me what's going on, because I should be sensitive enough in the spirit to pick her up. You have to have your mind on somebody other than you in order for that to happen. She stretches out her hand to the poor. When's the last time that you were at the store and you saw that someone didn't have enough money so you gave them the extra that they needed to be able to pay for their bill? When's the last time you felt led to give someone some money for gas while they were standing at the counter, whether they had enough or not. A virtuous woman is not just concerned about herself and what she can do for herself. She's not just concerned about making sure she has food in her house, gas in her car, and necessities for her kids. She's looking out for her neighbor. Look out for your neighbor Virtuous Woman!

## Busy But Balanced

We already know that we as women have 900 things on our lists. I do too - I probably have 920 and you probably have 922. We have to learn how to balance all of that. We must learn how to be what God has called us to be. There is no excuse for you not to fulfill what God has given you to do. We can make up excuses all we want to, but God isn't hearing them. He isn't receiving any of our many excuses. You need to believe that. You can go to God with your excuses if you want to. It's not that this is a to-do list of things that God wants you to do. You know what God wants you to do because you feel it by conviction. We feel by conviction what God wants us to do, and when we're not doing it, our conscience condemns us for our disobedience.

I can't really read this verse for those who dwell in the warmer regions of our country, but verse twenty-one says that *"She is not afraid of the snow for her household: for all her household are clothed with scarlet."* Virtuous women aren't worried about a storm coming because they prepare for the storm. The Bible says that a prudent man sees the storm approaching and prepares himself (Proverbs 22:3). This virtuous woman is just that way. She can go outside and just tell that the storm is coming, and she'll go ahead and get her house ready. These are the craziest times we have ever lived in, and some of these women don't have a clue about anything. They're cute but they're crazy. Some of them are as dumb as a bag of rocks. They can't boil water. They can't make a pot of rice without a rice cooker. Question: How are you from down south and you can't cook rice without a rice cooker? You want a husband but you can't cook. No man wants to eat KFC every night. No man wants McDonald's and Burger King every night. Mothers used to teach the younger women how to cook if they didn't know how. They used to prepare young women to be wives. It doesn't matter if the mothers are only thirty - if that's what God put in the house, and they know how to make some rice and clean a house, you'd better sit down and listen to them. I'm not saying that cooking is all you need to know how to do, but you still need to know how to do it. You need to have something that you're bringing to the table. If you can't cook and brother can't cook, how are y'all gonna eat?

During the time of my first wedding anniversary, we were waiting for housing at Fort Dix. My husband volunteered to cook some dinner for me, and I was so excited. He went in the kitchen and fried some chicken - I can't remember what else he cooked because I couldn't get over the chicken. That's all I remember is the chicken. We sat down at the table and that chicken was beautiful! It was nice and brown and crispy. When I broke that chicken open, it just ran with blood. I shouted, "Oh my God! Let me go fix this." I give him credit because at least he tried. He can cook now, but back then...not so much! And if I didn't know how to cook, there would have been no celebration. We would have both been looking at each other crazy trying to figure out what we were going to eat.

Don't be afraid of the snow or of the storm that's coming. Be prepared. Stop waiting until the last minute for everything. Some of us are last-minute planners. We wait down until the last minute. Church starts at the same time every Sunday. Why haven't you set your clock? Why didn't you get gas the night before? You know you're supposed to be in place. I'm talking about being a virtuous woman. Most work schedules begin the same time every day. That means you need to take care of your responsibilities-that may include ensuring that dinner and home taken care of. Where is your preparation? Prepare yourself. What if your household is dependent on you, and you're out of place? What if you forget? What if you wait until the last minute? You can't do that and in the end, your home not suffer the consequences as a result.

## Modesty is Not Outdated

Verse twenty-two says that "*She maketh herself coverings of tapestry; her clothing is silk and purple.*" She has her body covered up. It's funny how we sit on the front row of the church and try to pull our hem line down. Baby, there isn't any more material there. You can't pull anything else. There's nothing left for you to pull. Get you a lap cloth or get you a longer skirt. I'm not trying to take you back to the dark ages, but I am trying to get you to cover it up. Don't nobody want to see all of that? Take that home and let your husband look at it. If you don't have a husband, you go home and look at it yourself. We don't want to see all that.

## Self-Neglect

The virtuous woman does not neglect herself. We need to talk about that because sometimes we as women neglect ourselves. We take care of everybody else and we're sick. We take care of everybody else and we're run down. We take care of everybody else and forget that we have a need. We make sure that Sally has pantyhose, we make sure that you have shoes, we make sure that you ate dinner, and then we forget to get these same things for ourselves. It is not the will of God for us to neglect ourselves. God isn't going to give you any brownie points because you left yourself out. You're not going to get any brownie points for coming to church with a fever. Stay home and take care of that. Your friends and family love you and want to see you, but if you're sick, they need you to stay home and get well. God isn't going to be mad at you because you were sick. There's no need for you to come to church and bring us all your germs. Then we can't call on the elders of the church because they're all sick! Ask God to help you to stop neglecting yourself.

Sometimes you have to take a mental health day. I take mental health days. I love the sheets and the pillows at the Marriott. I love the sheets and the pillows at the Holiday Inn Express. Every once in a while, I go to visit. I love those covers. Sometimes you have to take a break so that you can hear yourself think. Why? Because you just did all of these things from verse ten all the way to verse twenty-two. You're taking care of everybody else. You're doing all of this stuff for everybody else, but you're forgetting about you. You can't help anybody if you're dead. You can't help anybody if you're sick. You can't help anybody if you're stuck in the hospital somewhere. You've got to learn how to take care of yourself. Put a coat on when you go outside. Cover up your throat with a scarf when it's cold. Learn how to exercise so that you can live longer. Why should we die before our time? These are simple things, but we often neglect ourselves.

## What Real Glory Looks Like

Verse twenty-three says, *"Her husband is known in the gates, when he sitteth among the elders of the land."* How is that? That's not from something he did - it's from something she did. From everything she did, she gave him a good name. Isn't it so in society today that when a woman is a mess, they talk about her husband as well? You have to understand that your godly behavior gives a good name to your whole house. Your ungodly behavior gives a bad name to your whole house. If you are a single mother, you aren't exempt - your kids are known by your behavior. The people at the school know that you're crazy and they warn people not to mess with you or your kids. That's just the way it is. We have to be virtuous women who are watchful of our behavior. We need to be women of strength who have good reputations. We need to be women who are good because we have the spirit of God inside of us. We have to make an effort to live holy. We have to make an effort to be good wives, mothers and businesswomen. We have to strive to be good Christians following after God. We can't just come to church just to say we did our "Christian Duty". There is a lifestyle requirement that accompanies our confession of Christianity.

Verses twenty-four and twenty-five tell us that *"She maketh fine linen, and selleth it; and delivereth girdles unto the merchant. Strength and honour are her clothing; and she shall rejoice in time to come."* It may not seem like it's your time to rejoice yet, but your time is coming. You'll be able to rejoice. Sometimes it seems like we are just working and that nothing is happening. It seems that we aren't making any headway nor are we getting any breakthroughs. The scripture says that you are going to rejoice in the time to come. You need to confess with your mouth that you will rejoice in time to come. Your time is coming. You might be crying now, but you won't be crying always. You might not be able to dance right now, but your day is coming in which you will be able to dance until your shoes wear out. Why? Because you're going to wait on God. And waiting on God is NEVER in vain, it ALWAYS pays off!

We learn in verse twenty-six that *"She openeth her mouth with wisdom; and in her tongue is the law of kindness."* This means that she's not talking a lot of dumb stuff. When you start talking, you shouldn't sound like a crazy goof ball. It's a shame. If you don't have anything in your head then you need to get something in your head. Pick up your Bible and read. In this age of the internet, no one should suffer from ignorance. Even if you can't read, there are audiobooks that will read to you. You are without excuse. A blind man is still able to hear the word of God.

## Occupied and Focused

Verse twenty-seven says that *"She looketh well to the ways of her household, and eateth not the bread of idleness."* She's not spending hours doing nothing. The rest of the chapter tells us that *"Her children arise up, and call her blessed; her husband also, and he praiseth her. Many daughters have done virtuously, but thou excellest them all. Favour is deceitful, and beauty is vain: but a woman that feareth the Lord, she shall be praised. Give her of the fruit of her hands; and let her own works praise her in the gates."*

This isn't a competition. It's what goes on in your house that matters. Whatever is going to work in your house, you have to make it work yourself. That isn't anybody else's responsibility. Don't be trying to come up in the church and get your pastor to work out your troubles. Go home and fix it. You might just have to go home and shut up. I have to go home and shut up sometimes. Let somebody else be right sometimes. We don't always have to be right.

If you want to know the secret of being a virtuous woman, you need to walk in the fear of the Lord. The Bible says in Psalm 111:10 that "*The fear of the LORD is the beginning of wisdom.*" This is why we don't have wisdom. We're not walking in the fear of the Lord. Concerning this virtuous woman - on the one hand, her husband's name will be good, and on the other hand, her works will speak for herself. We need to learn how to just get it together. We have to deal with ourselves. We have to learn how to love our neighbors as well as being industrious. We need to be industrious. We need to stop being lazy and making excuses. Get up out of that bed. I know there's just something about that bed that we love, but we need to make ourselves get up out of that bed and get moving. We should strive to be virtuous women. There is no excuse. Obedience to God should be our primary goal. We must be virtuous women. You may not have to sew anybody's clothes or plant vineyards, but you do have a vineyard in the spirit that you can sow into and reap from. You need to make sure that you take care of the vineyard God has allotted to you. God is holding you accountable. You should be able to come before God and lift up holy hands. Don't come in the church living one thing and go out living something else. The person we see you as in the church, at work, or in the grocery story is who we want to see every day. We don't want to relate to you as a stranger, because your behavior makes you unrecognizable. Ask God to make you a virtuous woman in every way. This is His will for you Woman of God.

# Girl Get A Grip: Business and Ministry Coaching Edition

# 8
# KEEPING YOUR HEART ALIVE

You can go through things that will kill your heart and your spirit, and take from you your vigor to live. Has anybody ever been there? I know it's not just women - there are some brothers who have been blindsided by some things in life and it has really torn them to pieces. We are going to talk about hurting women and hurting men. We need to deal with the fact that we need to learn how to keep our heart alive. This is something that the Lord has been dealing with me about. I never really took the time to go look up anything about it before because I just said to the Lord, "I just want my heart to stay alive." While I kept going through whatever it was that I was going through, I just kept saying, "Lord, I've gotta live through this. I can't let this kill me. I can't let this steal my joy. I can't let it steal my prayer life. I can't let it steal my vigor for life." I know that I have times where I'm quiet, but I like to laugh and have a good time with other people. I'm not talking about being carnal or anything like that - I just like to be happy. I don't know anybody who likes to be sad and miserable all the time.

When I did take the time to sit down and see what our Christian community say about our hearts being kept alive, I couldn't find anything. The Muslims have hour-long videos about how to keep your heart alive. The new agers have stuff out about how to keep your heart alive. We in the Christian community know that suffering is a part of our lifestyle if we are really Believers. If you're not suffering and you're a Believer, then we will need to talk about that later. As I began to look up information about keeping our hearts alive, I could only find music. I couldn't find any messages or videos from the church or to the church. Really, we are the ones who need these kinds of messages. We don't seem to understand that when we go through difficulties, we don't know how to go through properly. That's why we start turning to psychology and all of these other things to try to soothe our aching hearts - we don't know how to stay alive.

The Christian group Sanctus Real has a song entitled, "Keep My Heart Alive". When you look at the words to this song, it simply says in the beginning about how he is tired of politics and tired of getting bad news. He says, "I'm tired of chasing the moment instead of chasing You." What happens to us is that we start chasing after things. We start chasing after having something. We try to keep up with the Joneses and the Smiths and the Browns, and all of the rest of these other people. We sit next to Prophet Doohickey at church and they seem like they have it going on. It looks like everything is together in their life, and we don't understand why we are still struggling. We listen to some of the prosperity preachers and they make us think we are supposed to have it together all the time. They make us feel like our bank accounts are always supposed to be overflowing and that we are always supposed to have the best whip (for the younger people), cars (for the older people). When we don't have those things, we feel like God is not with us anymore. I'm here to tell you that the Bible says that when you suffer, the spirit of glory and of God rests upon you.(1Pe.4:14) If you want to know how to get glory on your life, you need to go through. We need to go through. That's not popular for us because we want to hear "feel-good" messages. We want to come into ministry settings and have someone speak encouraging words and sing a couple of songs to us. We want to be told how good we should feel and how beautiful we are. Listen: You can get a mirror and tell yourself that. I need to explain to you how to make it through your adversity. Adversity is not going to leave you alone just because you crawl in a corner and cry. Have you ever tried that? I did. It didn't work. When I came out of the corner, guess what? My adversity was still there.

### Let's look at Matthew 6:19-23:

"Do not lay up for yourselves treasures on earth, where moth and rust[e] destroy and *where thieves break in and steal, but lay up for yourselves treasures in heaven, where neither moth nor rust destroys and where thieves do not break in and steal. For where your treasure is, there your heart will be also. The eye is the lamp of the body. So, if your eye is healthy, your whole body will be full* of light, but if your eye is bad, your whole body will be full of darkness. If then the light in you is darkness, how great is the darkness!"

I am a teacher by nature, and I want to be able to lay good foundation. We go to church, we holler and scream, and we leave with nothing. We yell, we foam at the mouth, we snot, we cry, and we don't even know what we're snotting and crying about. I want to make sure that when you put this book down, and if you have to face hell in your home, you will know how to keep your heart alive. Shouting is not going to help you keep your heart alive. Shouting for some of us is an open show that our heart is still living through what we are going through. That's how we try to encourage ourselves to keep our heart going.

The Bible tells us in Proverbs 13:12 that *"hope deferred makes the heart sick"*. We go through things because there are times when we are waiting for God to show up and do something, and because He doesn't show up in the way that we think He should, we become sick in our hearts. There are some things that I have been waiting for that I want God to hurry up about. I've been praying and fasting and crying and it doesn't matter how much I cry - it doesn't make it move any faster. I just thought I would help you out with that little sidebar. Your crying is not going to make God hurry up. You have to be able to endure, and make it through what you go through what you are facing so that you will have a testimony on the other side. When we talk about being our brother's sister and our sister's keeper, I cannot be a good sister to you if my heart is dead. I'm symptomatic of someone who is ill. Anybody who is dealing with heart disease or any kind of heart condition knows that they can't run up and down the street like anyone else.

They can watch others sprint and run around with everybody else but they can't do all of that because their heart is sick. If you actually have to sit on the sidelines to watch, though you desire to move, you can't move. That is part of what we are dealing with. Why am I using these verses of scripture and analogies? Because Jesus takes three chapters to talk the disciples and give them the constitution for the Kingdom of God. If we want to know what God's Kingdom consists of, we can read Matthew 5, 6, and 7. Really, that is the summation of our salvation. If you can't follow what's in there, you might as well hang it up. I'm not saying that you're not supposed to follow the rest of the book - I'm just saying that if Jesus is having a conversation with the disciples that lasts three chapters, that's important.

When we get to the sixth chapter, Jesus speaks to us about what our hearts are set on. These are the things that tend to deal with us. We come to church and we smile, but our heart is not where we are sitting. We go to jobs every single day and sit at desks, pick up telephones, drive down the highways, and our heart is not in what we are doing. Jesus is telling them that wherever their heart is, that is where their treasure is going to be. Then He goes from there to talking about light and how your perspective is on life. He's dealing with two things, actually. Jesus talks about the light in us being darkness. On the one hand, darkness will bring damnation to you, which is an eternal consequences for your heart not being right. On the other hand, there is a natural consequence. One analogy for this light has to do with happiness. It has to do with how you see things. It has to do with whether you are pessimistic or a "negative Nancy" in your perspective. We want to try to find another way because we don't want to do it God's way. We want to go lay on somebody's couch and let them tell us what we should do. Can I just get a pill so that I can let this go away? Can I drink it away? Can I get rid of this some other way? I want to tell you:our heart condition has everything to do with how we serve God.

When you look at the words to the song I mentioned previously, the writer talks about how he is in church saying empty hallelujahs. We can say the same. "I'm in church saying 'hallelujah' but it's not full of anything. There's no life behind it, there's no joy behind it, there's no power behind it - I'm just saying it because that's what everybody else is saying. You say 'Hallelujah', I say 'Hallelujah'. Everybody say 'Hallelujah'! This is what we have become. We have become the people who know how to operate by rote and auto-pilot. We have light in us, but the light that is in us is darkness. We are unhappy. We're not walking in the joy of the Lord.

There are things every day that are reaching after our affections and our love for God. This is why the scripture tells us to love the Lord with all of our hearts, minds, and strength (Deuteronomy 6:5). Why? Because this is about your perspective in life. Whatever you give your heart to has control over you. Why is it that a relationship with a man or a woman can break you down like nothing else? It's because your heart is in it. We have to learn how to deal with our hearts when they become sick. When we get sick in the physical, what do we do? We call the doctor or we go to the emergency room. In church, when our hearts get sick, we just come in and we gloss it over. We do our hair, we put our makeup on, and we make sure that everything is in order. We look good and we smell good, and we hope that nobody knows that our hearts are really sick. "I'm here, but I'm not here. I'm just taking up space, and my 'hallelujahs' are empty. Really, inside, I'm tired of all the politics in church. I'm tired of chasing after empty promises. I'm tired of sitting next to folks who don't know anything about me. They act like they're here with me but they're really not here. People say they're my sister or brother but are really my enemy. They just want my business so they can run down the street and tell somebody else." There are things that are symptomatic of us being sick in our hearts - but we're saved and we love Jesus and we're going to Heaven anyhow. I beg to differ. We have to deal with our heart issues.

Matthew 6:22 tells us that the lamp of the body is the eye. When you look at Ephesians 1:18, this is a reference to the heart. So for all of you Bible scholars who like to cross reference, there is one for you. Matthew 6:22 continues, *"if your eye is healthy, your whole body will be full of light, but if your eye is bad, your whole body will be full of darkness."* In other words, if your outlook isn't right, things won't be right. Think about the example of seeing the glass half full vs half empty. Perspective is everything. The way you see something will determine whether you are going to fight for it or whether you are going to lay down and die. How do I know? I've had to make those choices. I've had to decide whether I was going to keep fighting or lay down and just die. Do I feel like I want to lay down sometimes? Yes I do. But I refuse to, because I know that if I seek God, and if I stay in His presence, He will allow my heart to stay alive in the midst of what I'm facing. For some of us, when we come to church and nobody prophesies to us or prays for us, we think the word wasn't for us. We hope that God will speak directly to us. Maybe it's just that you couldn't hear Him. You can't tell me that God was speaking and it wasn't for you. There is a heart issue there that is preventing you from being able to receive that word. Instead of acknowledging that heart issue we want to blame the preacher and say that they should have prayed a little harder. If you're reaching out with you heart, and if you decide that you're hungry and you won't allow anyone to keep you from getting to what you need to eat and eating it, when the food is set on the table, even if you don't like the food, you will eat it if you're hungry.

Light is figurative of happiness and goodness. Darkness is figurative of unhappiness and ruin. This is what Jesus is talking to them about. He is talking to them about eternal consequences which we need to be focusing on. What we are understanding is that this is about Jesus. Our help is in Him. Our deliverance is in Him. If I give you platitudes and tell you what the latest psychologists and statistics are saying, I'm not helping you. For too long, we have been coming to church for psychology and looking for people to psychologize us and we're not understanding why we are still not delivered. No pun intended, I talk a little rough because that is the New York in me, but I have been wondering why we have all of these "Woman Thou Art Loosed" conferences and nobody is loosed yet. Woman you're bound when you get there and woman you're bound when you get home. I would want my money back! If I came here to get delivered, I need something to help me get delivered. Even if you don't want this food, I'm going to force feed you today.

You are going to get your money's worth. We get what we pay for. If you're just going for an experience with somebody's personality, then you go have all of that and the leftovers. But if you want to be delivered, you are going to have to look at what kind of light is in you. You're going to have to deal with what kind of thoughts are going through your mind when you are by yourself. What is it that you are telling yourself when nobody else is around? What are we telling ourselves? What are we listening to? What are we watching on the hellivision? These are all things that kill our hearts. We don't understand why we can't live and why we can't go through. We don't understand why we feel defeated. We feel like our prayers are hitting the ceiling and we can't seem to get a breakthrough. Breakthrough is waiting for you. Breakthrough is here for you - but you need to deal with your heart. We cannot treat God like He is a genie in a bottle. That's what we like to do. We like to turn around three times and tap our neighbor one time. We like to tell our neighbor that we are coming out and that this is our season. I don't want you talking to your neighbor - you need to talk to YOURSELF!

Because our hearts are sick, our relationships don't work. We can't get along with our siblings, we can't get along with mama, we can't get along with daddy, and we even leave our spouses. How do I know? Because I did that too. I was sick and tired of being sick of tired, but I had to check my heart. We are ready to point fingers but are we willing to point our fingers at ourselves? Are we willing to look at ourselves and say, "The problem isn't my neighbor. The problem is me. My heart is sick. My heart is beating, but there is a blockage. There is something keeping me from getting the air that I need. There is something that is preventing me from being able to breathe like I need to breathe. Life seems to be killing me and I don't understand why it's killing me. I have to be honest about what kind of light is in me. I love Jesus, but I'm full of darkness. I love Jesus but I don't feel like I have any hope. I love Jesus but I just can't see my way out." I like to tell the truth, the whole truth, and nothing but the truth so help me God. You know why? Because I'm tired of liars. I'm tired of the posers, the fakers, and the wannabees. I'm tired getting up and telling people that God is blessing and moving but I'm crying by myself. Tell the truth and say that you need someone to pray for you. We can't trust our brothers and sisters with our secrets so we walk around sick. We are scared that they will tell someone our business. How do I know? Because we tell each other's business when we don't know it. I had the rumor mill to hit my house. I heard some of the rumors and I knew that people were lying. I wasn't chasing any stories because I was concerned about my heart living through this. I had to sit down and hear God and say "God, what are You saying through this to me?"

When you get to the course of the song, it says, "Jesus, keep my heart alive." You can't do this by yourself. That's what's wrong with us. We try to do this by ourselves. We try to be Superman and Superwoman but they must die. You have to take your cape off, you have to get out of that invisible jet. We try to do everything and try to save everybody else but ourselves. What is that? Culturally speaking, as African-American women, we try to save everybody. We try to do everything, and we try to be everywhere. We try to help, help, help - but who is helping us? This is the self-help part of this message. Say, "Self, you have to take your cape off and deal with your heart. In Jesus' Name. Amen."

*Matthew 7:24 -27 (English Standard Version)*
*"Everyone then who hears these words of mine and does them will be like a wise man who built his house on the rock. And the rain fell, and the floods came, and the winds blew and beat on that house, but it did not fall, because it had been founded on the rock. And everyone who hears these words of mine and does not do them will be like a foolish man who built his house on the sand. And the rain fell, and the floods came, and the winds blew and beat against that house, and it fell, and great was the fall of it."*

Sometimes we are looking for a word from God. Let me help you. Can you follow the first block of instructions before looking for Him to give you the next block of instructions? You can't be looking for something extra when you didn't do the first part. The first thing He says in the 24th verse is that everyone who hears the words and does them... Can I take a quick side bar? We have to understand that "hearing" is not just hearing. Hearing is doing what you hear. If my kids didn't do something when I told them to do when they were growing up, they would say that they heard me, but they didn't' do what I said. I would commence to busting them up because they didn't do what I said. Don't tell me that you heard me if you didn't do what I said. So here's Jesus and He's talking and He says that if you hear these words and do them... Let me tell you how to build your house. You need a house that will stand. I have read this verse a million times, but as I read this verse again, I began to hear the Lord talking to me.

Verse 25 says that the rain fell and the floods came. The winds blew and beat on that house. That sounds like life to me. If you read the King James Version, it says that the rain descended. The rain descended and the floods came and the winds blew and beat on that house, but guess what? It did not fall... because it was founded on the rock. If you are going to keep your heart alive, you're gonna have to obey God. You will need to do what God says. You need to learn how to pick up your Bible even when you don't feel like reading. I have learned how to force feed myself. There have been times when I felt like I was going to die. There were even times when I thought about killing myself because I was fed up, tired, aggravated, and I felt like I didn't have anybody. I had to learn how to force feed myself. That's what they do to people in the hospital when they can't take care of themselves. They put an NG tube down their nose. If they stay immobile for too long, they have to cut a hole in their stomach and put a G tube in so that they can eat. You have to lay hands on yourself and tell yourself to eat. We are not at a deficit of eating food, but we are at a deficit of eating the Word. We are at a deficit of spending time in the presence of God so that God can equip us and empower us to be able to live. You've gotta understand that you can't live this life in your flesh and think you're going to walk in victory. It's not going to happen that way. People are going to walk away. People are going to talk about you. Your marriage may fail. Your family may not want to be bothered with you. The people at church may say, "We don't like you, your feet stink, and we don't think you love Jesus." They might talk about you all kinds of ways. You have to be able to feed yourself the Word even when you don't feel like eating. That's a hard thing to do. That's hard thing to do because when we don't feel like eating we just pick over our food. We don't want it. We are like that with our Bible reading as well. We say that we stay in our Bible but we are liars. God already knows. You're sitting at home crying. You're not reading your Word. I'm getting ready to tell you how I know.

*Verse 26 says, "And everyone who hears these words of mine and does not do them will be like a foolish man who built his house on the sand. And the rain fell, and the floods came, and the winds blew and beat against that house, and it fell, and great was the fall of it."*

Let's talk about what rain is. Jesus is so smart. I always tell the saints that they wanted to push Jesus off the cliff because He had a smart mouth. He was saying stuff and telling people off. Even though He talked in parables, He told people off. When they caught on to it after the fact, they would want to bust Him up. "Did He say that?" So here it is that He is giving them an analogy. Everybody understands everything about rain.

When it rains, nobody wants to get out of the bed. We want to stay in our pajamas. Can you hear what God is saying? He said the rain came. The rain fell. The rain descended upon that house. We go through, and life begins to rain on us. We don't want to get out of the bed. We don't want to take off our pajamas. We don't want to do our hair. Just because some of us can put a wig or a headpiece on doesn't mean that we comb our hair when we get home and take that piece off. We came in the house cosmetically covered, but our hair was matted to our scalp. Rain is a time of dreariness and depression. We want to shut the world out and we don't want to be bothered. Weather is a mood changer. It's a buzzkill. It's a fun snatcher. Don't plan on having a picnic in the rain because rain messes up everything. Who wants to eat a soggy sandwich? Nobody wants that. You want the sun to be shining, you want the weather to be right, and you want everything to be at the right condition. What Jesus is saying is that life is going to come against you and you have to make sure that you build your spiritual house right so that you can endure and stand the storms of life.

You can't sing "Happy" and thinks that's gonna change anything. Singing worldly songs will not make the sun come out. Happiness is a condition that is set upon something happening to make you happy. This is why the scripture tells us about the JOY of the Lord which is our strength. This is why you have to force-feed yourself. This is why you have to keep your heart alive. When it starts raining and you forgot your umbrella at home, and you don't have on any goulashes, and you are all dressed up and your make up is on fleek, you went through all of that stuff and you get rained on. Weather is a game changer. It changes things for us. The scripture says that the floods came. This indicates that people came against us. Some say,

"I would love going to church if it wasn't for the folks that are there." I like to say what everybody else thinks. We have large numbers of people who come against us. Even when I was writing this, I heard the Spirit of the Lord say that these are strategically-placed people who come to bring harm or overwhelm you in the midst of your circumstances. They come to fight you and make you feel like you are outnumbered, when really, you ARE the number. I'm telling you: perspective is everything. When you don't have your perspective right, you will be in the middle of battle and quit when you're standing right there at the finish line. When it looks like all hell is coming out against you, that's what the flood is. When you go and read the about the rain descending, that word "descend" means "to unleash or to let loose". It's like hell coming after you. Guess what? I can "book" that. The Bible says that hell beneath you has reached up after you (Isaiah 14:9).

You have to understand that if you're going to live for your circumstances and be able to breathe life in to someone else, can you please live for yourself first? When you are on a plane, they tell you that in the event of an emergency, the air mask will come down. They tell you to put the air mask on your first before you put on one on somebody else. How am I going to try to save you and I'm dying of asphyxiation? That is the picture of the church. We are dying and we're trying to save everybody else. It's foolishness. It's nonsense. It's pure folly. The Bible says that the winds blew and beat upon the house. What this means is that there is an unforeseen or unexpected force that comes against you. The Bible says in John 3:8 (King James Version) that "The wind bloweth where it listeth, and thou hearest the sound thereof, but canst not tell whence it cometh, and whither it goeth: so is every one that is born of the Spirit." So, this is telling me that this is an element that I cannot control. Honestly, that's just life in general. Unexpected things that you can't explain. People think you are cursed by God because of what you're going through. You don't know how to explain to them that you know that you are just going through something right now so that they don't look at you like you are crazy. I'm going to tell you: living is the best vengeance. Just live. Baby, just live. I don't care who's telling you to roll over and die. I don't care who is already printing out the programs for your funeral service - you better LIVE! I have a refusal to die. The Bible tells me that Jesus gave up the ghost. This means I have a say in this. I'm not giving up anything. I want my heart to stay alive. Do you want your heart to stay alive?

We have to be able to handle when these winds start blowing against us. The scripture says that the winds beat against the house. This speaks of being blindsided. These are events that come that just tear us up from the floor up. Stuff that brings you to your knees. Sometimes because you're just going along people think you're okay, not realizing that there are things going on in our hearts that we need to talk to somebody about. You shouldn't have to go to the psychologist to get help when you are sitting next to a spirit-filled believer. You mean to tell me that you don't have enough Holy Ghost to cast out a headache? You don't have enough Holy Ghost to cast out depression and oppression? You don't have enough Holy Ghost to command that heart to live? I need you to sit your Holy Ghost down. If your Holy Ghost doesn't work, I need to find some who has a working Holy Ghost power in their life. If we are going to be the church, we need to function like we are who we say we are. If the Son of the living God is living inside of us, why can't we let our hearts live through what we're going through? I don't care what kind of losses you suffer. I don't care who walks away. I don't care who you bury. You better let your heart live! God put us in the earth to accomplish His will. You're not here just so you can have 2.3 children, have a white picket fence, get a Mercedes Benz and be cute when you come to church. That's not your life function.

You are supposed to be salt and light. When we have things in our life that don't operate according to their function we get rid of them. We get rid of them because if you put something in place for a function, it must be able to be used for that function. If I'm a believer and the power of God is in me, I should be able to resuscitate ourselves first. We always want the mic so that we can preach to everybody else but we can't even bring life into ourselves. You don't need a mic, Smookie. Sit down and go get a prayer life. I need you to be able to resurrect you first. When I come to your service, and I see you resurrect you first, and I see you living and breathing and walking around, then you can lay hands on me. Until then, you can lay right there in your casket. You need to understand that sometimes us going through is not just God judging us. It is His chastening. We get up and we quote "who the Lord loves, He chastens" (Proverbs 3:12) as long as we're not being chastised. I have had to preach through some of my chastisement. I have cried my way to church and said "Fran, get a grip girl. Don't you go in there and give those people any of this. They need to hear your God." If you can't preach past your circumstances, you're not ready to preach. If you can't live beyond your circumstance, you're not ready for this. You have to be ready to breathe life into you. The Bible says that the husbandman is first partaker of the fruit (II Timothy 2:6). That's not just about money, honey. That's not just for blessings. You have to eat this word first. I spent the last five years eating this. I was on my face, groveling in the presence of God, asking Him to just let my heart live. "God, whatever is going on. I don't care who leaves me. I don't care how lonely I get. I don't care how bad it gets. Just let my heart live." David understood that. He said in Psalm 51, "Uphold me with your free spirit. Don't take Your Spirit from me." If You take Your Spirit from me I can't make it. That's what keeping your heart alive is. It's that the Spirit of God is still resident on the inside and it's working.

The wind has a drying nature (Genesis 8:1). Sometimes what I don't understand is that we go through things and we get tired because our trials come back to back. This is what Jesus is saying to them. The rain came, and then the winds came. We know that when the wind starts coming, it's bringing more rain. Jesus is telling them that they will experience rain and then the wind will come and dry you out. With that wind, will be more rain, and it's not the refreshing rain. It's the rain that brings more tests, more trials, and more people coming against you. The flood comes in because God is letting it rain again. Help us, Lord.

So how am I going to be my brother and sister's keeper when I don't have anybody to be a keeper for me? If I'm on auto-pilot all day every day, and I don't let God deal with my heart, how am I going to help somebody else? This is for preachers first. If we are preaching, we must have a heart that is alive. How are you going to preach to people that you have no feeling for other than feeling like you don't want to be bothered because they get on your nerves? You can't do it. That's not the right spirit. We all want the light, but we don't understand that when that light comes on, it's going to expose everything. This means that there is stuff you don't want anybody else to see that they will see. Can you handle that? Can you handle being under that microscopic light like that? How can I help anybody when I myself need help? We have to lose this mentality that as long as we have King Jesus we don't need anybody else. We have to be careful what we're singing. That's superwoman and superman mentality, and superwoman and superman must die, if you're going to keep your heart alive!

Girl Get A Grip: Business and Ministry Coaching Edition

# Thriving *Woman Coaching Journal*

*"Souls who follow their hearts thrive, fools bent on evil despise matters of the soul."*
*Proverbs 13:19 (MSG)*

Francesca Stubbs

# 9
# THRIVING WOMAN COACHING EXERCISES

## Chapter 6
## Shattering Perceptions: The Woman Question

Describe any faulty perceptions you may have had concerning your womanhood.

_____
_____
_____
_____
_____

List 3 things you learned as a result of reading this chapter.

_____
_____
_____
_____
_____

What is your opinion concerning Feminism? Do you agree or disagree with the ideology shared in this chapter concerning Feminism and its roots? Explain.

_____
_____
_____
_____
_____

Have you encountered challenges in ministry or life regarding your role as a woman? In what way have your challenges strengthened or discouraged your stand regarding your call to ministry?

_____
_____
_____
_____
_____

## Chapter 7
## Virtue, Women, and Reality T.V.

Do you believe the description of the Virtuous Woman in Prov 31 is too farfetched to attain? Why or why not?

_____
_____
_____
_____
_____

What images have you seen portrayed by Hollywood which cause you to be angry? Why?

_____
_____
_____
_____
_____

How would you apply the principles shared in this chapter to your everyday life?

## Chapter 8
## Keeping Your Heart Alive

Can you identify any heart-issues that you currently have? What are they and how do you intend to deal with them?

_____
_____
_____
_____

Are you always trying to save everyone else to your own neglect? Describe your personal support system.

_____
_____
_____
_____

Have you ever been blindsided by life's events? How did it affect your heart condition?

_____
_____
_____
_____

Francesca Stubbs

# Bibliography/ Citations

Chapter 3 Page 20;
discouragement.Dictionary.com. Dictionary.com Unabridged. Random House,Inc.
http://www.dictionary.com/browse/discouragement
(accessed: September 20, 2017).

Chapter 6 Page 32;
Feminism. Dictionary.com. Dictionary.com Unabridged.Random House,Inc.
http://www.dictionary.com/browse/discouragement
(accessed: September 20, 2017).

The Importance of Women Business Owners. Media Planet Article by Bruce Purdy, © 2017 Pg 4; (Accessed September 22, 2017)

Girl Get A Grip: Business and Ministry Coaching Edition

## ABOUT THE AUTHOR

Francesca Stubbs is a global speaker who has ministered on platforms in the U.S. and overseas. She is an Apostle in the Lord's church as well as a successful Entrepreneur. Her business acumen has allowed her the privilege to work in various sectors of the business world, providing mentoring, corporate counseling/coaching, as well as working with individuals to create nonprofit enterprises and education hubs.

She has appeared on various International Christian Television programs to share her testimony, talk about her books and preaching the Word of God. She currently travels the country providing ministry training, Increase Now Financial seminars for ministries and businesses as well as ministering the Gospel of Jesus Christ.

Francesca has been married to her highschool sweetheart, Javer for almost 30 years together, they are the proud parents of four (4) adult children: Jessica, Ijason, Javer Jr., and Francesca Darnelle

## Other Books and CD'S By The Author

The Battle of the Overcomer: A Spiritual Warfare Guide for the Believer
ISBN-13: 978-1469904160
ISBN-10:1469904160
BISAC: Religion/Christian Life/Spiritual Warfare

Girl Get A Grip: A Woman's Guide to Surviving Adversity (Handbook)
ISBN-13: 978-1499686234
ISBN-10: 1499686234
BISAC: Religion/Christian Ministry/General

Girl Get A Grip: A Woman's Guide to Surviving Adversity (Workbook)
ISBN-13: 978-1512164077
ISBN-10: 1512164077
BISAC: Religion/Christian Ministry/General

## Speaking Ministry

Francesca Stubbs is a Minister of the Gospel of Jesus Christ, Entrepreneur and Global speaker who travels the United States and the World carrying a message of Hope, Healing, and Encouragement for those in ministry as well as those in the business sector.

She is a seasoned Speaker, Life Coach and Mentor with a proven track record for producing measurable spiritual and natural results in the lives of those with whom she has come in contact.

Her rigorous ministry schedule includes various appointments for conferences, revivals, seminars, preaching and life coaching/empowerment sessions.

### Contact Info:
SODAAN GLOBAL
P.O. Box 229
Spring Lake, NC 28390
Office Phone: (910) 239-7923 or (910) 321-5964
Email: sodaanmedia@gmail.com
Website: www.sodaanglobal.org

### Connect with the Author on Social Media:
Facebook: www.facebook.com/apostlefran2014
www.facebook.com/SODAANGLOBAL
Twitter: www.twitter.com/ApostleFran

www.ingramcontent.com/pod-product-compliance
Lightning Source LLC
Chambersburg PA
CBHW070312230526
45470CB00002B/842